No Nap for Zack
and
Zack Gets Zapped

Level 3 – Yellow

Helpful Hints for Reading at Home

The graphemes (written letters) and phonemes (units of sound) used throughout this series are aligned with Letters and Sounds. This offers a consistent approach to learning whether reading at home or in the classroom.

HERE IS A LIST OF PHONEMES FOR THIS PHASE OF LEARNING. AN EXAMPLE OF THE PRONUNCIATION CAN BE FOUND IN BRACKETS.

Phase 3			
j (jug)	v (van)	w (wet)	x (fox)
y (yellow)	z (zoo)	zz (buzz)	qu (quick)
ch (chip)	sh (shop)	th (thin/then)	ng (ring)
ai (rain)	ee (feet)	igh (night)	oa (boat)
oo (boot/look)	ar (farm)	or (for)	ur (hurt)
ow (cow)	oi (coin)	ear (dear)	air (fair)
ure (sure)	er (corner)		

HERE ARE SOME WORDS WHICH YOUR CHILD MAY FIND TRICKY.

Phase 3 Tricky Words			
he	you	she	they
we	all	me	are
be	my	was	her

TOP TIPS FOR HELPING YOUR CHILD TO READ:

• Allow children time to break down unfamiliar words into units of sound and then encourage children to string these sounds together to create the word.

• Encourage your child to point out any focus phonics when they are used.

• Read through the book more than once to grow confidence.

• Ask simple questions about the text to assess understanding.

• Encourage children to use illustrations as prompts.

This book focuses on the phonemes /x/, /y/, /z/ and /zz/ and is a yellow level 3 book band.

No Nap for Zack
and
Zack Gets Zapped

Written by
Georgie Tennant

Illustrated by
Lily Fossett

Can you say this sound and draw it with your finger?

No Nap for Zack

Written by
Georgie Tennant

Illustrated by
Lily Fossett

Zack tells Mum to tuck him in.
He will nap.

Buzz! Buzz! Zack cannot nap.
He will fix the buzz.

Zap zap zap! He zaps the buzz.
Zack can nap.

Fizz! Fizz! Zack cannot nap. He will fix the fizz.

Zack gets a cup. It will fizz and hiss less.

Zack naps. Yap! Yap! Yap!
Zack cannot nap.

The dog is in the box! Zack will fix the yap.

The dog zigzags to bed. Zack and the dog will nap.

Zack naps. Zed yells. Zack will fix the yell.

Yum yum! Zack gets back into bed.
Buzz, buzz!

It is Rex! Zack will not fix this buzz!

Zack and Rex exit. No nap for Zack!

Can you say this sound and draw it with your finger?

Zack Gets Zapped

Written by
Georgie Tennant

Illustrated by
Lily Fossett

Zack is on Zipzap.

Zip! Zap! He zigzags to a big box.

Suck! Zack yells. He is in Zipzap. Max yells.

Max will fix this! Max will get Zack to the exit.

Max is on Zipzap. Zack is in Zipzap.

Max gets Zack to run. Max gets Zack to zap.

Zack zigzags. Max yells. Zack is not at the exit.

Zack is in a fix. Max gets him to zap the web.

Buzz! Zap! Max and Zack will win!
Max zaps the bad Zod.

Buzz! Zap! Max zaps and Zack zips.
Zack zaps the big Zig.

Yes! Max has got Zack to the exit. Suck!

Zack is not in Zipzap. Zipzap was fun!

©2022 **BookLife Publishing Ltd.**
King's Lynn, Norfolk, PE30 4LS, UK

ISBN 978-1-80155-471-8
All rights reserved. Printed in Poland.
A catalogue record for this book is available from the British Library.

No Nap for Zack & Zack Gets Zapped
Written by Georgie Tennant
Illustrated by Lily Fossett

An Introduction to BookLife Readers...

Our Readers have been specifically created in line with the London Institute of Education's approach to book banding and are phonetically decodable and ordered to support each phase of Letters and Sounds.

Each book has been created to provide the best possible reading and learning experience. Our aim is to share our love of books with children, providing both emerging readers and prolific page-turners with beautiful books that are guaranteed to provoke interest and learning, regardless of ability.

BOOK BAND GRADED using the Institute of Education's approach to levelling.

PHONETICALLY DECODABLE supporting each phase of Letters and Sounds.

EXERCISES AND QUESTIONS to offer reinforcement and to ascertain comprehension.

BEAUTIFULLY ILLUSTRATED to inspire and provoke engagement, providing a variety of styles for the reader to enjoy whilst reading through the series.

AUTHOR INSIGHT:
GEORGIE TENNANT

Georgie Tennant is a freelance writer who has written multiple stories for BookLife Publishing. She always knew she would be a writer as she used to present her school teachers with lengthy stories and poems for them to enjoy! Her two sons provide plenty of entertaining material for her writing, which usually appears on her blog or in the local newspaper as the 'Thought for the Week'. When she isn't writing she is working as a part-time secondary school English teacher, where she has the joy of inspiring slightly bigger children with the joy of reading good stories. She hopes to write good stories for them one day too.

This book focuses on the phonemes /x/, /y/, /z/ and /zz/ and is a yellow level 3 book band.